Tiny habits. Big change.

Atomic Affirmations for Success Habits is your go-to guide for rewiring your habits, one powerful step at a time.
This easy-to-use book distills the game-changing ideas behind Atomic Habits into bite-sized affirmations, mindset hacks, and journal prompts — designed to help you:

- Build success habits that stick
- Break free from old, disempowering patterns
- Take consistent micro-steps toward your goals

Are you stuck in a rut, repeating the same routines but craving different results?
Chances are, it's not a lack of effort — it's your habits and identity working on autopilot.
The good news? That autopilot can be reprogrammed.
You'll learn how to shift three key drivers of behavior:
Your Environment, Your Intentions, and Your Approach.

This book helps you change the script — not by overhauling your life overnight, but through practical, doable, and repeatable shifts that compound over time.

You'll discover:
- How to design your environment for effortless follow-through
- Why motivation isn't everything (and what works better)
- What to do when you fall off track — and how to bounce back faster
- Journal prompts that bring your inner wisdom to the surface
- Affirmations that rewire your mindset from the inside out

Whether you're starting fresh or refining your next level, Atomic Affirmations for Success Habits is a toolkit for anyone ready to step into more clarity, momentum, and meaningful change.

Let's be honest — most of us don't have time (or the focus) to read a full book from cover to cover.

That's exactly why Atomic Affirmations for Success Habits was created. It's made to meet you where you are — busy, motivated, and ready for change in bite-sized doses.

How to Use This Book
There's no one "right" way — choose what feels good for you:

- **Option 1: Flip and Flow**

Open to any page. Read the affirmation.
Then pause and answer the journal prompt — this is where the real magic happens.
Taking that small moment to reflect will anchor the insight deeper.
(And remember, we tend to repeat what we reward — even if that reward is just a spark of inspiration.)

- **Option 2: Start from the Beginning**

Move through each affirmation and journal prompt one by one.
This path builds strong momentum, helping you gradually reshape your habits and inner narrative from the inside out.
Whichever approach you choose, by the time you reach the end, you'll have built a more intentional relationship with yourself — and with the small choices that lead to big change.

Pro tip:
Make the most of the journal prompts. Your written reflections are the bridge between thought and transformation.

About the author

Roslyn Loxton, B.Coun, lives in Australia and wears many hats — entrepreneur, creative, mindset coach, emotional clearer, singer, sister, wife, aunty, friend, and devoted dog mum.

Since 2007, Roslyn has worked in the fields of mindset, psychology, emotional healing, and clearing, helping others move through their blocks and step into aligned, purposeful living.
A lifelong lover of music, singing continues to be one of her deepest expressions of joy and connection.

You can explore more of Roslyn's services, courses, and transformational programs by visiting:

https://www.instagram.com/roslynloxton/
https://www.facebook.com/roslynloxtonmindsetcoach
https://eramusic.co

Changes in your life

CAN be achieved

by making

tiny achievable tweaks

to your daily rituals

Re positioning your flight path

isn't a response to failure

it is an act of consciousness

Life is ever changing seasons

being nimble 'is the way'

Goals Journal

Taking stock and getting the ball rolling.
Write out <u>*as many*</u> of your daily habits and rituals,
useful or un-useful, as you can identify.
Just begin to notice what you notice.

_____

_____

_____

_____

_____

_____

_____

_____

_____

When it comes to your desires

dreams or goals

Take the big picture

and divide it into sections

and then

just slightly improve

each section gradually

consistently

consistency is your friend

Goals Journal

Name 3 - 5 of your daily habits or rituals that you can slightly improve upon.
What do those improvements look like?
What might get in the way of this? What would it take to overcome the obstacles?

_____

_____

_____

_____

_____

_____

_____

_____

_____

_____

Goal success can increase simply by making small achievable positive shifts in each action step of the goal

Like the stone mason chipping away at the rock its hard and seemingly impossible

but there is a dedication to the process

Goals Journal

Start here to identify your goals and try to begin to break your goals down into chunks.
All the when, where, what, why's and how's.
Just to start noticing and analysing yourself in terms of what motivates you and what blocks you.

_____

_____

_____

_____

_____

_____

_____

_____

_____

_____

Small improvements

consistently

can swell into

a full blown

wave of results

Hold strong to this wisdom

Commit to YOURSELF

SHOW UP for yourself

Goals Journal

What are some small improvements you can make in the spirit of self commitment and showing up for yourself in the short term, medium term and the long term?

_____

_____

_____

_____

_____

_____

_____

_____

_____

_____

Creating tiny rituals

that turn into

positive habits

will lead to

what feels like miracles

You have to keep showing up

for your yourself

You have to **keep focused** on

what your heart desires

Goals Journal

Where do you need to and where can you start to show up for yourself more?

_____

_____

_____

_____

_____

_____

_____

_____

_____

_____

The results of our tiny rituals

become bigger

as we repeat them

and they grow in effect

and they become truely

powerful because they become

our identity

Goals Journal

What part of your identity
holds you back from your hearts desires, your best self
and your best life?

_____

_____

_____

_____

_____

_____

_____

_____

_____

Small

positive changes

to daily habits

silently shape shift your life

staying the course

continuing to make positive

changes

is where we need to commit

Goals Journal

How can you be better at committing
to you goals and intentions and staying the course despite
the challenges and set backs?

_____

_____

_____

_____

_____

_____

_____

_____

_____

_____

When a plane shifts flight path

by 1%

you can not tell

but the end destination

will change radically

It's the same

for our life's destinations

When we change

our daily habits

by 1% each day

we change our destinations

Goals Journal

What are some life achievements and destinations you would like to aim for?

_____

_____

_____

_____

_____

_____

_____

_____

_____

A slight shift

in the right direction

in your daily rituals

can lead your life

to much more appealing

destination

A much more deliberate

soul led destination

Goals Journal

What are some slight shifts you can make now in a heart and soul led way
and how can you help yourself to continue to stick to them?

_____

_____

_____

_____

_____

_____

_____

_____

_____

_____

When you stir a hot beverage
you create a current
Success
is a current and a flow
you generate in your life
created by the accumulation
of useful daily habits
all joining forces
conscious habits might seem
hard to create
but
unconscious habits can act like
a bad spell

Goals Journal

What rituals in your daily life have the most impact on the current of influences in your life? In the spirit of creating success habits, what do you need to become unavailable for?

_____

_____

_____

_____

_____

_____

_____

_____

_____

_____

Start new rituals
that create a pathway
toward
your desired outcomes
and importantly
make those rituals
achievable
you'll love the self empowering
results

Goals Journal

Name some rituals you know you could build into your days that would lead you to better habits that would lead your life to more desirable outcomes.

_____

_____

_____

_____

_____

_____

_____

_____

_____

_____

Your outcomes
are the after glow
of your actions
Your rituals and habits
inform your actions
so creating useful habits
increases your chances
of creating a fulfilling
on purpose after glow

Goals Journal

Describe a fulfilling on purpose afterglow you'd like to create in your life. Write it out as an affirmation that has already come into reality. Then name your emotions and explain the gratitude you feel.

___

___

___

___

___

___

___

___

___

___

___

___

It's what we do
with consistency
that will produce
a repeated outcome
It's what we do
with consistency
that will produce
a repeated outcome
It's what we do
with consistency
that will produce
a repeated outcome

Goals Journal

What are you consistent with already and what are you needing more consistency with?
Name the subsequent rewards or costs and outcomes.

_____

_____

_____

_____

_____

_____

_____

_____

_____

Knowledge and skills
build up and expand us
it's not one learning
but rather a commitment to
life long learning
that creates genius
and transformation
and a formula for success
that you can repeat
and take with you anywhere

Goals Journal

What knowledge and skills do you already have and what knowledge and skills do you need to acquire. What will it take to go about acquiring them?

_____

_____

_____

_____

_____

_____

_____

_____

_____

_____

Breakthrough moments
are often the results
of many previous actions
which build up the potential
to unleash major change
Like that stone mason
Yesterday you consistently
working for today you
consistently working for
tomorrow you

Goals Journal

What can today you thank yesterday you for?
What does tomorrow you require from today you?

_____

_____

_____

_____

_____

_____

_____

_____

_____

_____

Seeking instant gratification can be the enemy
to building a collection of effective success habits
However
getting in those tiny wins
on a daily basis
is epically motivating

Goals Journal

What can you do today to acknowledge your daily wins big or tiny?
What message does today you have for yesterday you?
What message does tomorrow you have for today you?

_____

_____

_____

_____

_____

_____

_____

_____

_____

_____

Practice for practice sake
and one day
out of the blue
you become
an overnight success
Commitment and consistency
are at every victory

Goals Journal

What do you need to practice today to honour your on purpose goals and to serve your dreams and your tomorrow you?

_____

_____

_____

_____

_____

_____

_____

_____

_____

_____

From little things
big things grow
If a seedling
compared itself to the tree we'd
run out of trees
Start small
nurture nurture nurture

Goals Journal

Where do you compare yourself to others? How does this impact and effect you?
What promise can your make to yourself when it comes to the act of comparing yourself to others?

_____

_____

_____

_____

_____

_____

_____

_____

_____

_____

You build a house
following a plan
you lay
one brick at a time
until eventually
you have a house
You build a goal with a plan
and you create a network
of rituals and habits
that build up
one day at a time
until your goal is simply a result
of your rituals and habits
Your goal then
is not so much your goal
but rather
nurturing and building
your rituals and habits is

Goals Journal

What rituals and habits can you focus on
for your best outcomes, for your best life and to honour to
your goals and dreams?

_____

_____

_____

_____

_____

_____

_____

_____

_____

_____

The system

to winning a race

is doing something daily

to improve your fitness

and your focus

Do one small thing

But never do nothing

Goals Journal

What do you have to stop doing and what do you have to start doing to create a success targeted system in your days?

_____

_____

_____

_____

_____

_____

_____

_____

_____

_____

When we desire

to change a result

it is a sign

to revisit our big WHY

and to change

the systems and processes

or the habits and actions

that lead to those results

and

where humans are involved this

includes attitudes intentions

and will and focus

Goals Journal

What is your big WHY?
How can your connection to your big WHY inspire others?

_____

_____

_____

_____

_____

_____

_____

_____

Where attitudes align
the magic of synchronicity
does most of the heavy lifting
There will be no need to
micro manage or over control

Goals Journal

What can you reflect on when it comes to your own attitude?
How open are you to becoming able to create and to integrate with synchronicity?

_____

_____

_____

_____

_____

_____

_____

_____

_____

_____

When you improve
the ingredients
you improve the cake
When you improve
your process, habits, rituals
you improve your outcomes
You want it
you show up for yourself

Goals Journal

What do you need support with when it comes to improving your habits and rituals as *these* are your process for achieving your dreams, desires and goals?

_____

_____

_____

_____

_____

_____

_____

_____

_____

_____

Ultimately be committed to
the purpose
more so
than the outcome itself
that way
any number of roads
can lead to Rome

Goals Journal

What is your conscious awareness of the purpose, a purpose, your purpose when it comes to how you spend your time and how you live out your days ?

_____

_____

_____

_____

_____

_____

_____

_____

_____

Build a process
that you're inspired to do
so that you will do it
and
it will lead you
to your success
But don't over rely on
inspiration
You will always need
commitment and consistency

Goals Journal

What type of things light you up and inspire you when it comes to designing and creating a solid process to follow for how to spend your time and achieve your goals?

_____

_____

_____

_____

_____

_____

_____

_____

_____

_____

Goal setting
is creating desired finish lines
whilst a powerful set of
habits and rituals
will create a life well lived
and a whole repeatable system
for nailing your goals

Goals Journal

What informed your current daily rituals and habits? Where did they come from? How are they contributing to your heart-led goals and to you on-purpose way of living?

_____

_____

_____

_____

_____

_____

_____

_____

_____

_____

Having is evidence of wanting
At some level
in our subconscious patterning
we get what we expect
It pays to tidy up our expectations

Goals Journal

What do you have in your world as a behaviour or an outcome that you 'say' you don't want?
What part of your blocks or shadow self or subconscious might be creating alot of your desired or undesired reality?

_____

_____

_____

_____

_____

_____

_____

_____

_____

What we are most committed to
unconsciously
and
consciously
is ultimately
what we will achieve

Goals Journal

What are you most consciously committed to?
What do you suspect your subconscious
might be committed to?

_____

_____

_____

_____

_____

_____

_____

_____

_____

_____

Transforming your habits
will happen
when you develop
small achievable repeatable steps
that grow into a habit
over time

Goals Journal

What is one small achievable step you can introduce into your daily routines that over time could build into a full blown success habit?

_____

_____

_____

_____

_____

_____

_____

_____

_____

Habits
are like the building blocks
of your house
each one is a fundamental unit
that contributes
to the overall growth
of your building
Building it up
or
Tearing it down

Goals Journal

If your main habits were the building blocks of a house what would your say about the house?

_____

_____

_____

_____

_____

_____

_____

_____

_____

Small
achievable daily rituals repeated
and improved
bit by bit over time
become a true source of
profound self empowerment
Aim for consistency versus
'All or Nothing'

Goals Journal

Where do you have all or nothing thinking? Why does that part of you need to exist? How does it serve you and how does it sabotage you?

_____

_____

_____

_____

_____

_____

_____

_____

_____

_____

The biggest impact
that you can create
in your life
will be improving
your daily habits

Goals Journal

What habit do you have that is creating the biggest impact in your life right now?

_____

_____

_____

_____

_____

_____

_____

_____

_____

_____

Focus on
who you need to become
in order to achieve
the outcomes you desire
When you desire
a certain outcome
especially those big hairy
audacious goals
turn your intention toward
becoming the person
that lives in the way
you need to live
in order to achieve
that specific success

Goals Journal

How much do you feel like you are already the identity of the person who achieves the dreams your heart desires to achieve?

_____

_____

_____

_____

_____

_____

_____

_____

_____

_____

Your subconscious biases holds hands
with your subconscious beliefs
and
your beliefs
drive your actions
change therefore
is an inside job

Goals Journal

What beliefs do you have that might be opposing the outcomes you aspire to reach?

_____

_____

_____

_____

_____

_____

_____

_____

_____

_____

What drives your network
of habits and rituals
is
your network of beliefs
conscious and subconscious

Goals Journal

What type of beliefs do you know or suspect underpin and drive your network of habits and rituals?

_____

_____

_____

_____

_____

_____

_____

_____

_____

To change habits and rituals
that do not serve you
or
to change your results
explore
how to change those
underlying covert beliefs
that fuel them

Goals Journal

What do you need to believe in order to create
a lifestyle in alignment with your soul led desires?

_____

_____

_____

_____

_____

_____

_____

_____

_____

_____

When we desire
a new set of experiences
and successes
we often need to change
the identity we are operating from
who we believe we are
and
who we believe we are not
deserve to be questioned

Goals Journal

What can you observe about your opinion of your own identity. What parts of your identity drives you and what parts hold you back?

_____
_____
_____
_____
_____
_____
_____
_____
_____

Once a useful habit
or ritual
becomes natural to you
and is an embodied part
of your sense of self
and is your identity
you have yourself
a success habit
an empowered form of
internal motivation

Goals Journal

What are your current internal motivations and which ones support you to live as your authentic heart-led soul self. Which ones force you to wear masks and repress your true self?

_____

_____

_____

_____

_____

_____

_____

_____

_____

Goals
are more likely to occur
when you change
an externally focused statement
that you
want something
into an internal statement
that you
are something
Our 'I AM' will dictate
what levels we will reach to
Swap
"I want to climb"
into
"I am a climber"

Goals Journal

What 'I AMs' do you need to start affirming?
And what 'I AMs' do you need to stop buying into?

_____

_____

_____

_____

_____

_____

_____

_____

_____

_____

Lasting change
is a result of
identity change

Goals Journal

If you could have one wish in relation to your identity changing, what identity change would you wish for?

_____

_____

_____

_____

_____

_____

_____

_____

_____

Improvements
like goals
are only temporary
until they become
part of your 'I AM'
your ego
your identity

Goals Journal

What improvements to your 'I AM' are you committed to making?

_____

_____

_____

_____

_____

_____

_____

_____

_____

Your own behaviour
and
your judgement
of other people's behaviour
are both a reflection of
your subconscious
Make your subconscious
Conscious
This is a journey worth taking

Goals Journal

Reflecting on the way you judge yourself and they way you judge others, what does this say about your identity?

_____

_____

_____

_____

_____

_____

_____

_____

_____

If the change you desire
does not align
with your self identity
the conflict between the two
will challenge your success
Now you know this
You can resolve this

Goals Journal

Where do you have conflict between your identity and your desires? What can you do to close the gap and change the playing field?

_____

_____

_____

_____

_____

_____

_____

_____

_____

_____

It's important
and even difficult
to learn how to unlearn
and
release old ways
and yet
this is essential to change and transformation

Goals Journal

What do you need to unlearn and to stop being or doing?

_____

_____

_____

_____

_____

_____

_____

_____

_____

Repetition of a habit
ritual or behaviour
will help to
transform your identity
And
your will and intention
and focus

Goals Journal

In the spirit of committing to your soul and heart led desires, what one small step can you start to repeat today?

_____

_____

_____

_____

_____

_____

_____

_____

_____

_____

Repeated actions
will gather evidence
which helps your identity
begin to transform
Seek evidence
in your daily surroundings
that alerts your identity
you already *ARE*
the person who achieves
their desires and
keep building on that

Goals Journal

What can you start *seeking evidence of* in your life that will start to improve where you tend to focus and will also help to positively affirm you?

_____

_____

_____

_____

_____

_____

_____

_____

_____

_____

The most effective way
to change your 'I AM'
your ego identity
is to change the
focus and rituals
you repeatedly engage in
not all at once but
step by step
bit by bit

Goals Journal

What ritual or habit do you need to cease and what habit or ritual can you replace that with?

_____

_____

_____

_____

_____

_____

_____

_____

_____

_____

It's not what we do sometimes that matters
it is what we do consistently that will inform our outcomes
We all drop the ball
A success habit
is to pick it back up
It's easy to feel inferior
But don't let that stop you
Just keep swimming
backstroke if it helps

Goals Journal

Try to reflect and describe what will be different for you when you stick to what is most important to your change and success?

_____

_____

_____

_____

_____

_____

_____

_____

_____

_____

Ask yourself
who is the type of person
that can get the outcomes
you want
then go about
taking daily actions
this person would take
Find your own way
so you *will* stick at it
Set yourself up to succeed
Role models are essential

Goals Journal

Who is a role model for the way you want to live your life? What is it about them that you could embody or replicate to start making your desired changes?

_____

_____

_____

_____

_____

_____

_____

_____

_____

_____

Once you have a sense
of the type of person
you want to be
you can begin making changes
taking small daily steps
to begin to reinforce
this identity
because if nothing changes
nothing changes
and
we get what we put up with

Goals Journal

If you are really honest with yourself, what have you been putting up with? What has it cost you? What are the consequences of not changing?

_____

_____

_____

_____

_____

_____

_____

_____

_____

The cycle is
your habits
develop your identity
and then
your identity
develops your habits

Goals Journal

What cycles can you detect in your behaviours and habits? Emotional, mental, physical, energetic, spiritual.

_____

_____

_____

_____

_____

_____

_____

_____

_____

_____

Focus
on being the *type of person*
that achieves
your desired outcomes
Visualise what this looks like
and
what this feels like
Practice, practice, practice this
in your imagination

Goals Journal

Write a note with advice and support to your today self from your desired full potential self

_____

_____

_____

_____

_____

_____

_____

_____

_____

Sometimes
we need to change
an old belief
by developing
a new habit
because
we become our habits

Goals Journal

What is one belief that you would like to release? Where did it come from? What habit will support you to make real change in this instance?

_____

_____

_____

_____

_____

_____

_____

_____

_____

_____

Your brain
is designed to form habits
to reduce the load of thinking
so it looks to the past
to assume the future
We *can* consciously
interrupt this cycle
to improve our process
for our own
highly conscious evolution

Goals Journal

What past story or belief formed in the past
is sabotaging your dreams, goals and desires for your life?
Or what evidence does your automation system seek to tell
you that you can or can't achieve something?

_____

_____

_____

_____

_____

_____

_____

_____

_____

At the root of all behaviour
are our primal drives
survival
safety
reproduction
so there is much more
to our behaviours
than surface level desires

Goals Journal

If you sit still and tap into your deeper self and with your deeper thoughts and feelings, ones that might otherwise get pushed back down and not acknowledged, what can you detect that might have a deeper more primal effect on your choices than you realise?

_____

_____

_____

_____

_____

_____

_____

_____

_____

Because the brain
is a reward seeker
it automates a cycle of
associations and cravings
that unconsciously prompt you
to take certain actions
Deepening self awareness
and
raising your consciousness
is key to your self mastery
and success

Goals Journal

What behaviours and actions could you start to build in some rewards for in order to encourage your brain to hand over to your automation system to work in your best favour? We repeat what we reward.

_____

_____

_____

_____

_____

_____

_____

_____

_____

Your cravings are
on automatic pilot
Mindful reflection of
what 'state'
the craving is seeking
is a powerful awareness
in spotting and interrupting
an unhelpful automation
Therefore raising your self
awareness
and self-empowerment

Goals Journal

Reflecting on your cravings, especially the ones that undermine your goals the most, what can you understand about the 'state' they are seeking to create within you?

_____

_____

_____

_____

_____

_____

_____

_____

_____

The cue
that sets off the craving
is where the problem area is
A change
in the way you respond
to that craving
is your self mastery
your power play
Removing cues is wise

Goals Journal

Reflecting on your cravings, can you identify what the actual CUE is that triggers the craving/s?

_____

_____

_____

_____

_____

_____

_____

_____

_____

When we raise our
conscious awareness
of our own cues (triggers)
and the subsequent cravings
and behaviour patterns
the beginning moments
of self mastery
have arrived
Making the unconscious
conscious

Goals Journal

What unconscious signals are you now noticing about yourself? How curious are you about the potentials for your life with increased self master?

_____

_____

_____

_____

_____

_____

_____

_____

_____

You have to feel it
to heal it
name it to change it
and
bring a non conscious pattern
out of the shadows
and into the light
to tame the beast

Goals Journal

What do you feel you need to heal and what will this free you from?

_____

_____

_____

_____

_____

_____

_____

_____

_____

Raise consciousness
Check in daily
and ask yourself
is this habit or ritual
supporting you
or sabotaging you
and
when might you be ready
to make a different choice

Goals Journal

Sometimes it's hard to even realise what some of our habits are. Try to name 3 habits that support your best self and 3 habits that sabotage your best self?

_____

_____

_____

_____

_____

_____

_____

_____

_____

Try talking
someone you care about
into taking on one of your
bad habits
and see how real
it suddenly becomes to you

Goals Journal

What bad habit are you most committed to breaking free from? What has it been costing you? What will this mean to your future to overcome it?

_____

_____

_____

_____

_____

_____

_____

_____

_____

_____

Creating clarity
by writing a plan
into your calendar
identifying how and when
you will start to form a habit
will greatly increase
the probability of
following through on the plan
It's the same
for taking vacations
Creating clarity
enhances your likelihood of
taking action

Goals Journal

What can you write into your calendar right now so that the universe can start getting to work teaming with you to help you to reach your goal? What can you start adding into your calendar?

_____

_____

_____

_____

_____

_____

_____

_____

_____

Hope
has it' own energy
and is a fuel to motivate
Nurture hope
Nurture anything that you want
to grow

Goals Journal

Where do you feel you need more hope? What is your relationship with hope? What might allow you to expect and invite more hope as a part of your identity?

_____

_____

_____

_____

_____

_____

_____

_____

_____

_____

Once you repeat a habit
often enough
it becomes a part of
your automation
and you develop
an unconscious competence
a powerful internal expectation
and
we generally get
what we expect

Goals Journal

Where do you feel you already possess unconscious competence and where would you like to develop more unconscious competence?

_____

_____

_____

_____

_____

_____

_____

_____

_____

Behaviour is always
at the mercy of environment
Create an environment
that encourages
desired behaviours
Remove temptations that
sabotage
Include tempations that
support

Goals Journal

In the spirit of setting you up for success, what temptations do you need to remove and what temptations do you need to include?

_____

_____

_____

_____

_____

_____

_____

_____

_____

_____

Carefully
pick the time and place
to start your new habit
and attach positive associations
to it
to give it the best chance
at becoming
a part of your daily routine
permanently

Goals Journal

If you were to carefully choose a time and a place to start a new habit, what would the action be and when will you take it?

_____

_____

_____

_____

_____

_____

_____

_____

_____

_____

Team your desired habits together
creating a springboard
for the next positive habit
and be specific
about when and where
your habits happen
Ambiguity is the pathway
to procrastination

Goals Journal

What are multiple habits to could team together, so one could springboard off of the other?

_____

_____

_____

_____

_____

_____

_____

_____

_____

Sure up
your environment
physically
emotionally
mentally
spiritually
energetically
because environment is more powerful than motivation alone

Goals Journal

Brainstorm all the ways you could 'sure up' and improve your environments to give you the best chance at sticking to your goals? What to remove and what to add in?

_____

_____

_____

_____

_____

_____

_____

_____

_____

You can design
your environment so
what you notice and see
makes it easier to
partake in your desired habits
Design your habit
as opposed to
merely consuming what is
already there

Goals Journal

What is it in your environments that is something you didn't design or choose but you are continuing to be hijacked by it? What can you do to overcome this?

_____

_____

_____

_____

_____

_____

_____

_____

_____

Increase your chances
of how many times
you'll think about
your desired habit
throughout the day
by deliberately placing
clear and obvious cues
around you that
encourage you to engage
in desired habits
and deliberately removing cues
that would encourage a
negative habit

Goals Journal

What are some negative cues you could remove from your environments now or soon and what are some positive cues you could add in immediately or soon?

_____

_____

_____

_____

_____

_____

_____

_____

_____

_____

The majority of us
live in an environment
full of random cues
created by someone else

Goals Journal

What are random cues around you now
set up by someone else? What can you do to change them
up for your best chances at success?

_____

_____

_____

_____

_____

_____

_____

_____

_____

_____

Redesigning your environment
to have new cues
that lead to a positive habit
makes it is easier
to build a new habit
in a new context
not competing with
old triggers and cues
Create zones
to support specific activities

Goals Journal

What ever the space it is you have to work with, what type of zones could you create to support your actions and positive habit forming behaviours?

_____

_____

_____

_____

_____

_____

_____

_____

_____

Bad habits
can come to a speedy halt
if there is
purpose built change
in the environment

Goals Journal

What can you say about your connection to purpose? What might some purpose built change look like?

_____

_____

_____

_____

_____

_____

_____

_____

_____

_____

Will power
is unreliable
the right environment
is king

Goals Journal

What can you notice about your own will power?
When is it reliable and when is it compromised?
What am I going to do differently?

_____

_____

_____

_____

_____

_____

_____

_____

_____

Concentrate on creating
a disciplined environment
and
the will power will emerge

Goals Journal

What might a disciplined environment look like for you? At work and at home? Allow yourself to contemplate and focus on your success and promise to keep showing up for yourself. Even if you do have wobbles now and then.

_____

_____

_____

_____

_____

_____

_____

_____

_____

_____

Because
of how neural pathways work
you can
break a bad habit
but it is unlikely
you will completely forget it
learn to *tune into*
the thoughts that
empower your resolve
train yourself not to negative
spiral and give up

Goals Journal

Think about the concept of 'tuning in' to thoughts and feelings, what do you notice about your own relationship or responses to what you 'tune into'?

_____

_____

_____

_____

_____

_____

_____

_____

_____

_____

We don't erase
old mindset pathways
we build new ones
and make them stronger
than the old ones
with repetition

Goals Journal

What old habit have you so far not been able to break?
What thoughts specifically feed the old habit?
The wolf that wins is the wolf we feed.

_____

_____

_____

_____

_____

_____

_____

_____

_____

Don't rely on self-control
rely on positive cues
and
purpose built environments
removing old cues that
encourage old habits
because avoiding temptation
has more success
than resisting it

Goals Journal

What can't you resist?
What would it take to avoid this?
How can you set yourself up to succeed?

_____

_____

_____

_____

_____

_____

_____

_____

_____

When our brain knows
it is going to get a reward
it is more likely to participate
in the behaviour
because desiring something
is more motivating
than liking something

Goals Journal

Describe the difference between desiring something and liking something in your opinion?

_____

_____

_____

_____

_____

_____

_____

_____

_____

_____

An extra level
of self mastery
is the ability
to team
what you like to do
with what you want to do
with what you need to do

Goals Journal

Try to write out a plan that teams what you like to do with what you want and need to do?

_____

_____

_____

_____

_____

_____

_____

_____

_____

The people
we are around the most
are the people
whose habits we will mimic
so hang out with people
who have the behaviours
you are trying to build

Goals Journal

Who are the people that you need to hang out with?
Who are the people you need to stop hanging out with?
Visualise the version of you who has successfully created
these changes and tap into their characteristics for help.

_____

_____

_____

_____

_____

_____

_____

_____

_____

New habits
will seem achievable
when we see
evidence around us
that others are also
doing them daily
Birds of a feather
flock together
for better or worse

Goals Journal

Where are the groups or who are the groups you would most benefit by becoming a member of?
What can you do today to initiate joining a specific group? Let yourself realise how vital this is to your growth and development and start by taking tiny steps in the best direction.

_____

_____

_____

_____

_____

_____

_____

_____

_____

_____

A powerful motivation
is belonging to a group
who are achieving
what you admire
and what you
desire to achieve yourself

Goals Journal

Remind yourself here what it is you want to achieve?
What will it mean to you to your life to achieve this?
How committed are you to sticking to the path?

_____

_____

_____

_____

_____

_____

_____

_____

_____

If you graze with a
flock of grazing sheep
you are more likely
to identify
as a grazing sheep
as our identity is
reinforced when we are
inside teams and groups

Goals Journal

What group has most reinforced your identity? What is that identity? How does it support or sabotage your heart-led on purpose life and goals?

_____

_____

_____

_____

_____

_____

_____

_____

_____

_____

Associate with people
who's positive behaviours
will influence
your behaviours
your future you
will thank you
Good associations
foster positive habits
Just like
Bad associations spoil
useful habits

Goals Journal

Write a note here from future you to today you about what was at the root of all your successes?

_____

_____

_____

_____

_____

_____

_____

_____

_____

_____

Life feels reactive
to the degree
that you are unconscious
so the more conscious
you become
the more predictive
your life becomes

Goals Journal

How reactive do you feel you are?
What does it mean to be 'conscious' to you?
How consciously do you feel you create your life?

_____

_____

_____

_____

_____

_____

_____

_____

_____

You can
predict your future
by looking at
your behaviours
and habits
and identifying
what they are linked to
or associated with

Goals Journal

What does your future hold given your current habits?
What have your unconscious habits cost you,
in all the ways?

_____

_____

_____

_____

_____

_____

_____

_____

_____

_____

If we are
endlessly predicting
what will happen
in our next moments
it makes powerful sense
to be doing this
from the identity
of your desired self
and not from
your not desired self
We are practicing
being our identity
every waking moment
Strive
to interrupt unhelpful patterns
of your 'not desired' self

Goals Journal

What identity shifts do you need and want to make?
What will this mean to your life and relationships?

_____

_____

_____

_____

_____

_____

_____

_____

_____

A craving
is a signal that says
in this moment
I want
to change how I'm feeling
We let the craving
make our choices
or
we ride out the craving
and
make a more conscious choice
We can choose to take a more
conscious action

Goals Journal

What are some of your unhelpful cravings and what are some ways you could ride the craving wave until it passes? Knowing this conscious action will create new resolves and inner strengths.

_____

_____

_____

_____

_____

_____

_____

_____

_____

_____

It is the signal of the emotion
that allows you
to mark things
as feeling appropriate
or feeling inappropriate
Start to notice and name
the emotions

Goals Journal

Describe your connection to your feelings and how you understand and process your feelings?
Start to notice if your feelings match your thoughts.

_____

_____

_____

_____

_____

_____

_____

_____

_____

_____

We are more attracted
to a habit
when we team it
with feelings
of positivity

Goals Journal

What might teaming a positive feeling with a positive habit look like for you?
Where can you implement this conscious process starting today?

_____

_____

_____

_____

_____

_____

_____

_____

_____

_____

We really are the creators
of our own world
we can find evidence for
what ever perspective or
belief or story
we are immersed in
Make this work in your favour

Goals Journal

When we wake in the morning, our mind unconsciously searches for our identity. What story or perspective do you continue to seek evidence for but it actually does not serve your desired identity or goals?
If you could, what part of your identity would you stop tapping into?

_____

_____

_____

_____

_____

_____

_____

_____

_____

_____

It is easy to get stuck
or emotionally hijacked
by the pursuit of 'perfect'
or the fear of making an error
but one step
in a forward positive direction
is all we need to take each day
teamed with a mindset that
looks for the evidence
that our positive habits
are yielding positive outcomes
Strive for the stars
But alway treat youself as
your own best friend

Goals Journal

What can you write about your pattern of seeking evidence for your outcomes? What is your usual 'go to' evidence seeking vibe? eg. You feel anxious so you look for evidence of what you are anxious about. Or maybe, you look for where you are unworthy or not enough.

_____

_____

_____

_____

_____

_____

_____

_____

_____

_____

If you want
to master anything
create a habit of taking action
and of practice
it strengthens your brains
pathways
Creating brain pathways
is how a habit is created
Don't give up
Change tact

Goals Journal

What do you need to stop practicing?
Who are you when you make conscious choices for your best self? What blocks you from behaving from this conscious identity all of the time?
How can you dissolve this block?

_____

_____

_____

_____

_____

_____

_____

_____

_____

_____

It doesn't take time
to create a habit
it takes repetition

Goals Journal

What really is your relationship with time?
If time was a person, how do you treat time?
How does time work for you and against you?
What would be the best relationship with time?

_____

_____

_____

_____

_____

_____

_____

_____

_____

Because people are wired
toward
the law of least resistance
create an environment
where building a desired habit
is easy
achievable
or even inevitable
remove the resistance points

Goals Journal

What is the hardest part about taking actions that lead to your best life and your ideal dreams and goals? What internal habit seems to trip you up or block you?
Can you contemplate your resistances and start kindly and curiously chatting with that part of yourself?

_____

_____

_____

_____

_____

_____

_____

_____

_____

_____

Create a routine
where
doing the right thing
is totally possible
by noticing and
removing blocks or obstacles
that rob energy and focus

Goals Journal

What do you feel your biggest obstacles are when it comes to creating routines that support your desired goals and life direction?

_____

_____

_____

_____

_____

_____

_____

_____

_____

_____

Create your environments
so that it is easier
to form good habits
and harder
to form bad habits

Goals Journal

If a group of psychologists were asked to come in and observe your environments, what do you think they might feedback about what your environments say about you?

_____

_____

_____

_____

_____

_____

_____

_____

_____

_____

Become aware
to your behaviours
small and large
as the unconscious habits
actually inform
the conscious choices

Goals Journal

Try giving the pen to your shadow self, or to your subconscious, or the parts of you that others don't get to see. What does this part of your psyche have to say about your goals and your rituals and habits? Try not to block or edit yourself. Be honest and curious.

_____

_____

_____

_____

_____

_____

_____

_____

_____

Shifting a bad day
into a good day
can be achieved by making
conscious deliberate choices
that lead you toward
your desired outcomes
Lead from conscious decisions
to 'tune into' what brings you
relief, groundedness, purpose

Goals Journal

What are some thoughts and ideas that you can build into your tool kit that help to bring you comfort and relief and re-setting if you do get hijacked by negativity?

_____

_____

_____

_____

_____

_____

_____

_____

_____

_____

Our habits
are leading us
to our outcomes
it pays to create
effective habits
from a place of deep self-worth

Goals Journal

What is going to change for you when you know YOU ARE WORTHY of every desire that's in your heart and soul?

_____

_____

_____

_____

_____

_____

_____

_____

_____

_____

Your day
is determined by
a myriad of choices
you have made
all stacking up
and the feelings
you have tethered
to their outcomes
be more mindful of this
so you can be more masterful
Do your thoughts
match your feelings

Goals Journal

What is going to change for you when you come to realise the person creating your reality is YOU?

_____

_____

_____

_____

_____

_____

_____

_____

_____

_____

If you wish
to create a new habit
make it achievable
to start with
and achievable
to sustain
Fear of failure is a distraction
Practice being bigger
than distractions

Goals Journal

Describe you and your life when you can feel fear in your mind and body but you don't let that stop you from making conscious well intended choices and actions?

_____

_____

_____

_____

_____

_____

_____

_____

_____

Getting started
on a new and useful habit
is usually harder
than continuing that habit
take the first step
take the second step
forward momentum is required
even if at first its in a slightly wrong direction
go for forward momentum

Goals Journal

What is stopping you from starting that desired habit?
What part of your internal resolve would benefit by having the volume turned up on it?
How do you turn the volume up on those positive internal voices?

_____

_____

_____

_____

_____

_____

_____

_____

_____

_____

Master the habit
of knowing
you can trust yourself
to show up
self-abandonment anxiety and
self limit
is what happens
when your not present and
connected and attuned with
your own 'real self'
with your own knowingness
Change 'I don't know'
into
At some level, I do know

Goals Journal

Where and when and how have you been abandoning your self?
What can you say to forgive yourself and to make a powerful new promise to stop self-abandoning and to stop seeking validation from external sources before you nurture your self validation first?

_____

_____

_____

_____

_____

_____

_____

_____

_____

_____

Fill your day up
with as many micro steps
as possible
that confirms *you are*
the person
you desire to be
you do create engaging rituals
that make it desirable
to partake of your consciously
chosen habits
One minute of conscious action
is better than none

Goals Journal

Where are all of your good serving habits that are already in place? Who is it within you that has embodied these positive habits? Where else can this part of you show up for yourself?

_____

_____

_____

_____

_____

_____

_____

_____

_____

_____

The effects of doing nothing
is negatively potent
therefore
it is better
to do one small thing
in the direction
of your desires
than to do nothing at all
Going to the gym
for 2 minutes
is better
than not going at all
Tomorrow go for 3 minutes

Goals Journal

What can I do today toward my goals that is creating motion, a tiny step in the right direction?

_____

_____

_____

_____

_____

_____

_____

_____

_____

Start off inefficiently
but start
and allow your self
the grace
to improve with time

Goals Journal

When it comes to fear of failure and or perfectionism, where do you stand and how is this stand serving and sabotaging your desires and goals?
What might a bit of self forgiveness and grace do for you?

_____

_____

_____

_____

_____

_____

_____

_____

_____

_____

Decrease
the number of steps
between you
and your positive habits
and increase the numbers
of steps
between you
and your bad habits

Goals Journal

What are some ways that you could make it harder to partake of the things that don't serve you and your best life and your best wellness and your heart-led goals?

_____

_____

_____

_____

_____

_____

_____

_____

_____

_____

Consistency is your friend when
creating
a new habit
and seeking
a transformation
Do something with regularity
however small as it builds your
identity
As opposed to abandoning your
intentions and doing nothing
as this erodes your identity

Goals Journal

What is it in your life and habits and behaviour that erodes your identity? What is it in your life and habits and behaviour that builds your identity up?

_____

_____

_____

_____

_____

_____

_____

_____

_____

_____

Attaching pleasure
to a behaviour is helpful
when forming a habit
it teaches your brain
to repeat that behaviour
because
we repeat what is rewarded
and
avoid what is punished

Goals Journal

Work out a reward system for taking even the most micro step in the right direction when building a new habit and also for ceasing an old un useful habit? Oh and also for building in rewards.

_____

_____

_____

_____

_____

_____

_____

_____

_____

Tether positive emotions
to positive habits
and
reward the desired behaviour
immediately
because what is celebrated
or rewarded
is more likely to be repeated

I keep reminding you of this

Goals Journal

What does tethering positive choices and actions to positive emotions look like for you, how can you do this in your life?

_____

_____

_____

_____

_____

_____

_____

_____

_____

The tricky part
about negative habits
is they can be
easy to engage in
delivering instant gratification
and yet
they have a delayed
negative consequence
making them
easy to partake in
in the moment
You can be bigger than this!

Goals Journal

Describe yourself when you *have empowerment* over the unconscious reward seeking trigger that tries to tap into instant gratification behaviours?

_____

_____

_____

_____

_____

_____

_____

_____

_____

_____

Creating micro feelings
of success
capitalising on small wins
will feed your desire
and
teamed with developing
a good relationship
with delayed gratification
are powerful behaviours
for self mastery

Goals Journal

List out micro feelings of success that you can lean into now you are conscious of needing them?
How can you improve your relationship with delayed gratification?

_____

_____

_____

_____

_____

_____

_____

_____

_____

Reward yourself
for avoiding
a bad habit
Get some advocates to cheer
you on for this too

Goals Journal

What bad habit can you avoid as of now and what is a reward you can build in to attach a positive association every time you choose well?

_____

_____

_____

_____

_____

_____

_____

_____

Developing transformation
takes multiple shifts
and approaches
Create yourself incentives
for starting positive habits
and build in
as a part of your identity
the intuitive sense
those habits
are natural to you

Goals Journal

Write out a page from the perspective of your empowered identity' and let that part of you suggest incentives for starting and keeping wisely chosen habits?

_____

_____

_____

_____

_____

_____

_____

_____

_____

_____

Keeping a track
of your progress
is backed by research
to say it increases
your chances of improving
as seeing progress
is highly motivating

Goals Journal

We can get stuck looking into where our gaps are instead of where our progress is.
List out all the progress you have made when it comes to developing yourself and your life, consciously?

_____

_____

_____

_____

_____

_____

_____

_____

_____

Aim for consistency
Perfectionism
can induce
'all or nothing' thinking
which can hijack
your delayed gratification
strategy
When you drop the ball
pick it straight back up
Dropping the ball is less a failure
than not picking it back up

Goals Journal

Write out some thinking around your delayed gratification strategy to help build the pathways in your brain and to have some handy touch stones or 'go tos' at any stage of your progress process? Especially for when the going gets a bit tough.

_____

_____

_____

_____

_____

_____

_____

_____

_____

_____

Focus matters
Measure your progress
YES
and stay focused
on *the purpose* of the goal
not the measures

Goals Journal

What are some helpful and maybe even some 'out of the box' ways that you can measure your progress so you can get those little victory buzzes that keep you motivated even on the struggle days, especially on the struggle days?

_____

_____

_____

_____

_____

_____

_____

_____

_____

_____

At some level
an unconscious level
an unproductive belief or habit
may have protected us
from a pain or a fear
Releasing this old behaviour
then
requires creating a *safe feeling*
replacement behaviour

Goals Journal

Describe what comes up for you around the concept that an old behaviour can be present within you as an old protection mechanism? Can you identify any of these within yourself?

_____

_____

_____

_____

_____

_____

_____

_____

_____

Creating a 'habit contract'
states
what the habit/behaviour is
and
also what the consequences
are for
not following through
Accountability
is a great motivator

Goals Journal

Write out an accountability contract that is designed to build in positive motivation and state which behaviours you want to be held accountable for and what consequences will be attached to not following through.

_____

_____

_____

_____

_____

_____

_____

_____

_____

_____

Attaching
a negative association
with a negative habit
is how the brain
will try to automate
avoiding
that habit or behaviour
(its why people who are trying
to become non smokers flick
them self with a rubber band
whenever they think of
smoking)

Goals Journal

Getting really determined here, what negative association can you attach to a negative habit to give yourself the best opportunity at avoiding a negative habit or behaviour?

_____

_____

_____

_____

_____

_____

_____

_____

_____

_____

Because we are designed
to work in collectives or tribes
setting up accountability
and being observed by others
is a powerful technique
for creating motivation
So long as its 'purpose built'
and not an old limiting
fear of judgement

Goals Journal

Where can you build in public accountability to support your desired behaviours, be it family or group or team accountability?

_____

_____

_____

_____

_____

_____

_____

_____

_____

_____

To increase your chances
for success
when in building a new habit
you align it
with your natural desires
and skills
One technique alone
won't work for everybody
Find what works for you

Goals Journal

What does aligning a new desired habit with your natural desires and skills look like for you at the moment?

_____

_____

_____

_____

_____

_____

_____

_____

_____

Comparing
ourself to others
can be an unsatisfying
unproductive behaviour
Compare-itis
We are better to be guided by
what feels authentic
and genuine to our own true
blueprint nature
Often being different is your
power play and
is more authentic and in flow
than
aiming to be better
or the same as others

Goals Journal

What are your authentic tendencies and where can you give these tendencies more appreciation by ceasing to compare yourself to others but rather delighting in your authentic differences?

_____

_____

_____

_____

_____

_____

_____

_____

_____

_____

Specialise in the areas
of your niche
skills and natural tendencies
especially
where they spark joy
and passion
You *can* be the master
in a narrow category

Goals Journal

Where can you be the master in a narrow category? As opposed to thinking you have to be the master of a broader category.

_____

_____

_____

_____

_____

_____

_____

_____

_____

_____

The more you understand
the truth of yourself
and stop comparing
the more
authentically you can
live your life
in all the ways
Which feels like flow and bliss
compared to push and shame
and fear

Goals Journal

Where are all the places that you can stop comparing your self to others starting from right now? What if you didn't care at all what other people thought of you when you are living from your authentic wisdom self.

_____

_____

_____

_____

_____

_____

_____

_____

_____

The golden rule
staying motivated
in life and work
is made up of
not too hard
not too easy
just right

Goals Journal

What would having more flow and balance look like for you if we could just click our fingers and create it right now?

_____

_____

_____

_____

_____

_____

_____

_____

_____

_____

Make a new
habit or behaviour
achievable to establish
and then continue to grow
and develop that habit
bit by bit by bit
so it continues to motivate
challenge and also deliver

Goals Journal

No growth and development is a one trick pony or a set and forget journey.
It is a constant reflection and re adjustment.
Everything is seasonal.
How is your relationship with reflection and re adjustment?

_____

_____

_____

_____

_____

_____

_____

_____

_____

_____

Be the boss of boredom
build in novelty
as boredom is inevitable
and
it can easily
hijack your resolve
and your focus
and your success habits

Goals Journal

When do you tend to stop a positive habit or behaviour due to boredom and how can you build in mini recharge points to ride the waves of boredom?

_____

_____

_____

_____

_____

_____

_____

_____

_____

No habit
will stay interesting
or effective forever
you have to be inspired by
your bigger why
and your bigger vision

Goals Journal

What is your bigger WHY and your bigger vision that will help to keep you motivated when boredom comes to visit?

_____

_____

_____

_____

_____

_____

_____

_____

_____

_____

Build consistency
as your habit
so you will show up
for yourself
despite your wavering moods
and motivation levels

Goals Journal

How will your relationship with yourself be different when you are no longer a slave to the habit of instant gratification and no longer open to giving up?

_____

_____

_____

_____

_____

_____

_____

_____

_____

_____

It is better
for your self mastery
to swap a habit
than to quit a habit
quitting
sends a disempowering
message to your self esteem

Goals Journal

What do you see for yourself when you know you can negotiate with swapping old unhealthy habits with new healthy habits as a super power of yours?

_____

_____

_____

_____

_____

_____

_____

_____

_____

Fall in love
with why
you're doing the work
in the first place
then despite changing
circumstances and wavering
moods
you can always find a how

Goals Journal

Tapping into your deepest heart of hearts, what vision for your life will help to keep you committed despite the distractions that come along to visit us all on a daily basis?

_____

_____

_____

_____

_____

_____

_____

_____

_____

Course corrections
are inevitable
be flexible and firm
review and reflect
and use your core values
and your conscious vision
your inner knowingness
as your guides

Goals Journal

Spend some time here writing about your core values as these will create a foundational grounding for all of the challenging decisions you will need to make in your life?

_____

_____

_____

_____

_____

_____

_____

_____

_____

_____

The more attached we are
to our identity
the harder it is for us
to let go of habits
that reinforce our identity
even if
it is our goal to do so
Be prepared to unlearn
and relearn yourself

Goals Journal

What part of your identity do you struggle to retrain and how does your preferred goal identity feel in your gut and in your heart and in your mind?

_____

_____

_____

_____

_____

_____

_____

_____

_____

_____

To the degree
that we are not self aware
we are vulnerable
un-well
The antidote to this
is self reflection
and targeted self development
from the soul self
not the ego self

Goals Journal

How can you tell the difference within your self as to which parts of your actions, habits and behaviours are your ego self and which parts are your soul self?

_____

_____

_____

_____

_____

_____

_____

_____

_____

_____

We have many facets
to our identity
and
to our daily rituals
small changes
in all of these facets
creates a movement
of transformation
in a conscious direction
bit by bit

Goals Journal

How can you embrace the spirit of bit by bit by bit in the right and consciously chosen direction?

_____

_____

_____

_____

_____

_____

_____

_____

_____

The more we reflect on
and refine
our personal systems
and processes
the more we identify
as successful
The more we identify
as successful
the more we reflect on
and refine our systems
and processes
Success is a habit
not an outcome

Goals Journal

How do you see your personal systems and processes? How are they working well for you and where are they tripping your progress up?

_____

_____

_____

_____

_____

_____

_____

_____

_____

Goals Journal

What have been your insights and breakthroughs by reflecting and journalling and becoming more conscious?

_____

_____

_____

_____

_____

_____

_____

_____

In the spirit of supporting self published authors
Please leave a review of this book

Keep an eye out for
A-Z Crystal Bible
Coloring in Book
and
Affirmations Journal

Goals Journal

_____

_____

_____

_____

_____

_____

_____

_____

_____

Goals Journal

_____
_____
_____
_____
_____
_____
_____
_____
_____

Goals Journal

_____

_____

_____

_____

_____

_____

_____

_____

_____

Goals Journal

_____
_____
_____
_____
_____
_____
_____
_____
_____

Goals Journal

Goals Journal

_____
_____
_____
_____
_____
_____
_____
_____
_____

Goals Journal

_____

_____

_____

_____

_____

_____

_____

_____

_____

Goals Journal

_____

_____

_____

_____

_____

_____

_____

_____

Goals Journal

_____

_____

_____

_____

_____

_____

_____

_____

Goals Journal

_____

_____

_____

_____

_____

_____

_____

_____

_____

_____

Goals Journal

_____

_____

_____

_____

_____

_____

_____

_____

Goals Journal

_____

_____

_____

_____

_____

_____

_____

_____

_____

Goals Journal

_____

_____

_____

_____

_____

_____

_____

_____

_____

Goals Journal

_____

_____

_____

_____

_____

_____

_____

_____

_____

Goals Journal

_____

_____

_____

_____

_____

_____

_____

_____

www.ingramcontent.com/pod-product-compliance
Lightning Source LLC
Chambersburg PA
CBHW071231070526
44583CB00017B/2129